Rags to Riches

The Craft of
Fabric Sculpture

Rags to Riches

The Craft of Fabric Sculpture

Irene Grant

Search Press

First published in Great Britain 1995

Search Press Limited
Wellwood, North Farm Road,
Tunbridge Wells, Kent TN2 3DR

Photographs by Search Press Studios
Photographs © Search Press Ltd. 1995

ISBN 0 85532 798 7

*To my husband Alan for his support and
understanding, to my family and friends for
their encouragement, and to my grandchildren
for their inspiration.*

Printed in Spain by Elkar S. Coop, 48012 Bilbao

Contents

Introduction 6

Materials and equipment 7

Figurines 10

Choirboy 10 • Angel 22 • Shepherd 24

Victorian-style Father Christmas 25 • Victorian lady 26 • Laundrywoman 28

Balloon seller 29 • Scarlett O'Hara 30 • Knight's lady 31

Bottle-based figurines 32 • Accessories for the figurines 38

Mounting your figurines 39

Decorative accessories for the home 40

Vase with tassels 40 • Mirror 44 • Calico candlesticks 45

Calico baskets 48 • Plaited garland 53

Calico cabbages 58 • More ideas 62

Index 63

*I*ntroduction

Fabric sculpture is a truly fascinating craft: recycling old fabric to make something new, creative and desirable.

With a few basic techniques, you can easily make a wide range of beautiful figurines and decorative accessories for the home using inexpensive everyday household materials and only minimal craft skills.

My first introduction to fabric sculpture came several years ago, when the local floral society arranged a one-day course on this subject. I had no idea what to expect and with an open mind decided to go along for the day. I was asked to bring some old cotton sheeting, wallpaper adhesive, a box of man-size tissues, a ball of wool, some newspapers, and some chicken wire!

My immediate reaction was one of disbelief – how could these basic materials be used to create attractive sculptures?

Of course, I made some entrancing things that day, and since then research and experience have allowed me to develop even more exciting ideas, using similar techniques. This book shares them with you, using easy-to-follow step-by-step photographs and pattern diagrams.

Please read this book in the same spirit and become, as I was, amazed at the results and well and truly hooked on fabric sculpture.

A candlestick created by simple fabric sculpture –
see pages 45–47 for how to make it.

Materials and equipment

Materials

Fabric

Old cotton sheeting is very suitable for this craft. Use medium-weight cotton or calico. Muslin is also very good for draping, but you will need double the amount. If you are going to spray your figurine with paint, as I generally do, it does not matter what colour or pattern you use.

If you are simply going to spray them with varnish, small-print cotton – for example dress fabric – would also be suitable. (Keep the scale of the pattern in proportion with the scale of the figurine – the smaller the figure the smaller the print will need to be.)

Charity shops, jumble sales and various fund-raising events can be a good source of suitable materials.

PVA (polyvinyl acetate) glue

Although this is a glue and is widely used in many schools, for craft work it is also excellent, when diluted with water, as a stiffening agent for fabric. Mixing it with one part water, pour into a large jam jar and shake well. Then pour it into a plastic bowl, ready for dipping your fabric. (If you have sensitive skin, you might like to wear thin plastic gloves when working with PVA.)

PVA drying time depends on how thick the layers are: for example, the figurines take about three days in a warm dry place, such as an airing cupboard or boiler room.

The baskets, garlands and vase, etc., take two days to dry.

Wallpaper adhesive

For the best results use the type of wallpaper adhesive which is used for hanging heavy-duty wallpapers.

Follow the mixing instructions on the packet and mix to a medium consistency.

To make one figurine, you will need about 2 litres (3½ pints) of adhesive. Allow at least two weeks' drying time for a really hard finish.

Wire

You will need some chicken wire (it must be galvanised to prevent it rusting). You can buy this from your local DIY or garden centre in a 10m (33ft) roll 600mm (24in) wide with 2.5cm (1in) mesh. Perhaps you could share a full roll of wire with a friend.

You will also need some 1.5mm (¹/₁₆in) thick plastic-coated wire for the arms on the figurines. It usually comes on a 15m (60ft) roll.

Paint

For most of the projects in this book, I have used acrylic and aerosol cellulose car sprays. For the garlands, I have used aerosol colour spray, which can be bought from most craft shops.

Should you decide not to colour your sculpture, do make sure you give it a protective coating of clear car-spray lacquer (two coats).

Wool

You can use up odd balls of knitting wool – plain or bouclé – for making wigs. To get a really hard finish, use: wool (100 per cent); mohair (100 per cent); and crochet cotton (100 per cent) – all of medium thickness. Man-made yarns are not so good for this purpose because they are very much less absorbent than natural ones.

Basic materials

1. Fabric
2. PVA glue
3. Galvanised chicken wire
4. Spray paint
5. A large box of man-size tissues
6. A packet of wooden plant-support sticks –
   about 30 x 1cm (12 x ½in)
7. Large newspapers
8. A roll of cellulose tape 2.5cm (1in) wide
9. A reel of strong button thread
10. A reel of cotton sewing thread
11. Plastic-coated wire
12. A ball of wool
13. Wallpaper adhesive

Other materials

To make some of the items in the second half of the book, you will also need

Small bag of sand
Large plastic sweet jar
Self-hardening modelling clay
Brass paper fasteners
Small bag of straw (for garlands)
Plastic plant pots, small and medium size
One or two plastic washing-up-liquid bottles

Equipment

The equipment you will need for this craft is neither expensive nor hard to get hold of: in fact, much of it will probably already be in your home.

1. One large pair of sharp scissors and one small
2. Long-nosed and snub-nosed pliers
3. Bradawl (for piercing holes)
4. Rolling pin
5. Wire cutters
6. Large plastic bowl for mixing adhesive
7. Tape measure
8. Darning needle (for wig making)
9. A selection of smaller needles
10. A turntable if you have one (or a large plate)
11. An old shirt or apron to protect your clothes
12. Pencil
13. Plastic sheet to protect your work surface.

Figurines

Everything in this book is quite simple to make. Although there seem to be lots of stages, you will find that you get much faster when you have made a few items and have got into the swing of making them.

First of all, I am going to show you how to make a basic figurine – a choirboy. The other figurines are only variations on this figure, dressed in different ways and with different accessories: the basic shape is much the same. So when you have made this first figurine, you will be able to make any of the others.

Choirboy

To make the choirboy, you will need the following items.

Materials

PVA glue or wallpaper adhesive
A plastic bowl for mixing PVA or wallpaper adhesive
1.5m (1½yd) of 90cm (36in) wide cotton sheeting or medium-weight calico
A ball of wool
A box of man-size tissues
Three or four broadsheet-sized newspapers
A small reel of 1.5mm (¹⁄₁₆in) plastic-coated wire
A section of galvanised chicken wire about 48cm (19in) square
A plant support stick about 28/30cm (11/12in) long and 5/10mm (¼–½in) thick
Cellulose tape 2.5cm (1in) wide
Strong button thread
Sewing cotton

Equipment

Scissors
Snub-nosed pliers
Long-nosed pliers
Darning needle
Medium-sized sewing needle
Wire cutters

Making the basic figurine

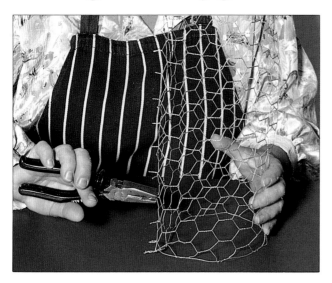

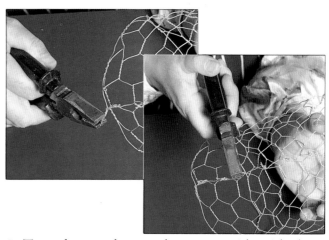

1. Using your wire cutters, cut the chicken wire to the required size. Snip through the mesh. This should leave two wire lugs. Now take the two ends of the wire section and join to form a cylinder. Using the snub-nosed pliers, twist the wire lugs to secure the join.

2. Turn the very bottom lug to one side with the pliers.

3. Turn the other lugs to lie flat along the joined edge.

Now make up the PVA by diluting it half-and-half with water. (Or use wallpaper adhesive – about 2 litres (3½ pints). Mix according to the instructions on the pack and set aside to thicken: it should be of a medium consistency.)

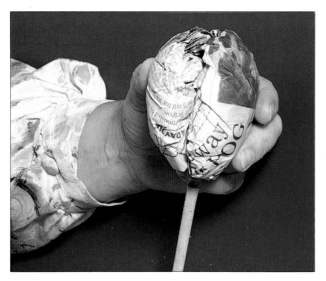

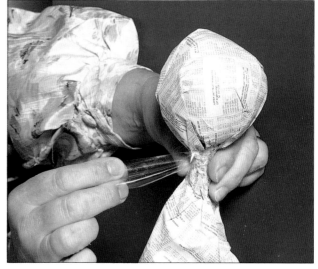

4. To make the head, take a double sheet of newspaper and tear it in half. Scrunch one sheet up into a half egg shape, compressing it into your hand. Repeat until you have two halves. Now take the plant stick and place it between the two halves of the head, gripping them tightly.

5. Place another sheet of newspaper over the head, supporting the two halves. Squeezing into the neck with your fingertips, bind the neck with cellulose tape as tightly as you can.

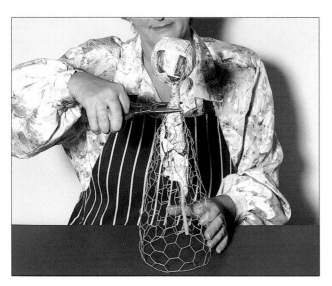

6. Now take the cylindrical wire frame you made earlier and form it into a cone shape, leaving a small hole at the top. Take the paper head on the stick and push it into the top of the cone. With the long-nosed pliers, grip the wire tight, leaving about 5cm (2in) exposed for the neck.

7. Next, cut two pieces of the plastic-coated wire 51cm (20in) long. Take one piece and mark the centre, then loop it around the neck. Repeat so that you have two lengths of wire either side.

8. With the snub-nosed pliers, start to twist the two wires from the base of the neck, continuing to the end of each arm. Loop at the ends to form hands. You now have the foundation of your figurine.

9. This stage is to give your figurine some stability. Tear a whole sheet of newspaper in half, screw it up, and push it up inside the wire frame. Making sure that the stick remains in the centre, pack tightly and fill to the base with crumpled newspaper, keeping the base flat rather than rounded.

10. Take out one tissue from the box of man-size tissues and tear it down the centre horizontally. Fold each half of the tissue in to a width of about 2.5cm (1in) to make a bandage.

11. Dip your fingertips into the diluted PVA. Lay the strip of tissue on the base of the neck and wind it down the arm, keeping it fairly tight and moulding it with dampened fingertips as you go. Repeat for the other arm, then build up the shoulders with more tissue. The idea is to cover the whole wire frame, first with the tissues and then with strips of cotton.

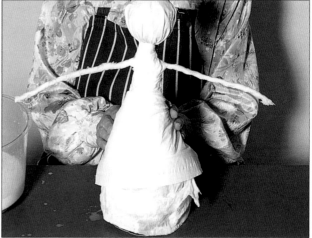

12. Now that you have covered the arms, take a whole tissue and place it over the head. Keep it dry, except for the neck (you will need to dampen the neck), squeeze and mould.

Using another tissue, criss-cross the chest area.

13. Continue covering the frame with tissue until it is completely covered, again by moulding with dampened fingertips.

Now cut out the pieces for the frame and the robes (see page 17) from cotton sheeting or calico, omitting the yoke, which you will cut to size at a later stage when you can see the exact size and shape of the area it is to cover.

14. Using the pieces of fabric now, continue covering the figurine. Take the face, smaller bandages, larger bandages, and base cover (see page 17). Dip the smaller bandage into the diluted PVA or wallpaper adhesive, soak well, and squeeze out, as with the tissues. Cover the arms, keeping the bandages fairly tight. Keep the hands tidy and small (one layer only).

15. Dip and squeeze the face square, and place it on the front of the head. Pull it taut and smooth it, taking any excess toward the back of the head, which will not be seen when the wig is in place. Dip and squeeze the smaller bandages, and wind them round the neck, keeping them tight. Also criss-cross the chest with bandages, just as you did with the tissues.

16. If you have a turntable, the sort used for icing, it will be a great help from this stage on, but if not, a large dinner plate will do just as well (to raise the hem of the figurine's gown off the tabletop).

   Dip the base cover into the adhesive, squeeze it out, and lay it over the turntable or dinner plate. Then pick up your figurine under the arms, place it in the centre of the turntable, and pull up one corner at a time, pulling fairly tight, then smooth it down.

17. Carry on dipping the larger bandages into the PVA, squeezing them out and using them to cover the rest of the frame.

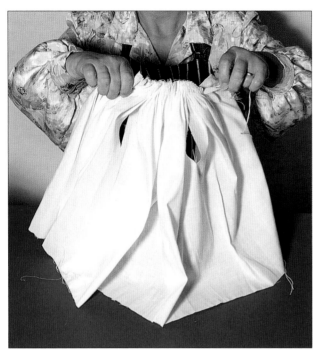

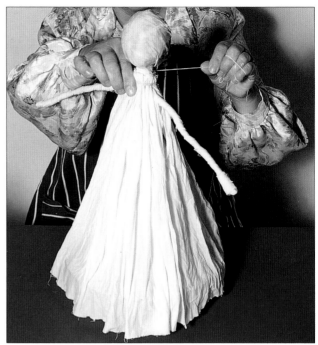

Making the robe (pattern piece A)

18. Cut the slits marked on pattern piece A about 3cm (1⅜in) from the top. These are to allow the arms to go through. Next, about 2cm (¾in) down from the top, sew running stitches about 1cm (⅜in) long from one end to the other. Knot one end of the thread.

Draw up the thread to gather the fabric and roughly arrange the folds.

19. Now dip the robe into adhesive, soak well, and squeeze out the excess. Put the arms through the slits and then draw up the threads finally.

With the opening at the back, overlap the two parts of the robe, pull the thread as tight as you can, tie off and knot.

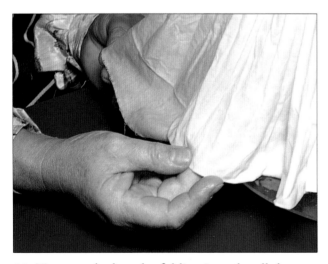

20. Turn up the hem by folding it under all the way round. The hem should touch the ground when the robe is extended.

21. Now for the really fun bit: simply pull and tweak the robe to form attractive folds. These will harden as the glue dries and will become permanent.

Pattern pieces for choirboy's clothes

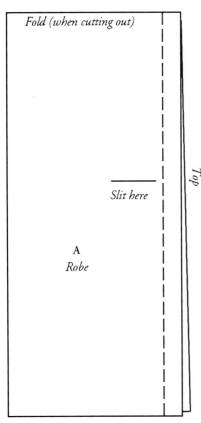

Fold (when cutting out)

Slit here

Top

A
Robe

1m (40in) x the desired height
of the choirboy

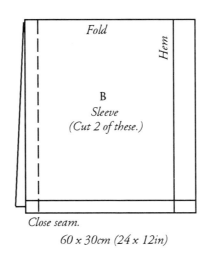

Fold

Hem

B
Sleeve
(Cut 2 of these.)

Close seam.
60 x 30cm (24 x 12in)

Fold

C
Ruff

56 x 12cm
(22½ x 5in)

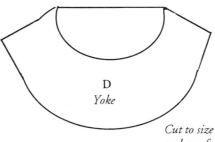

D
Yoke

Cut to size – one for the front
and one for the back. The
front neckline is more scooped
than the back.

Calico pieces for covering the frame

Face: cut a piece of calico
    12 x 12cm (5 x 5in)
Smaller bandages: cut 10 of these,
    30 x 2.5cm (12 x 1in)
Larger bandages: cut 10 of these,
    20 x 15cm (8 x 6in)
Base cover: cut one of these,
    35 x 35cm (14 x 14in)

– – – – – – – – – – = *running stitches*

(Diagrams not drawn to scale.)

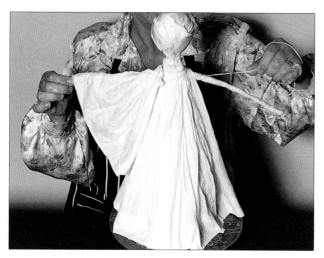

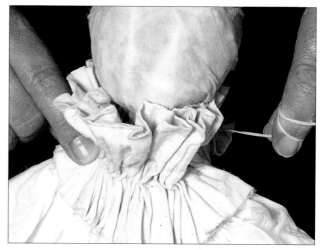

The sleeves (B)

22. Measure the figurine's arms from the base of the neck to fingertips, then add 3.5cm (1³⁄₈in) for the sleeve hem. Now close the underseam, secure at each end, and turn right side out. Using button thread, sew running stitches across the top of each sleeve and draw up the threads to gather the fabric. Dip the sleeve into the adhesive, squeeze out the excess, then place it on the arm. Making sure the seam is under the arm, draw up the threads as tightly as possible, taking the end of the thread across the back and winding it around the other arm to stop the sleeve from sliding down the arm. Repeat for the other arm.

Making the ruff (C)

23. With the fold as shown in the diagram, using button thread sew running stitches 2.5cm (1in) from the top (*i.e.* from the fold). Draw up the threads to gather the fabric, dip the ruff into adhesive, squeeze out the excess, place it round the figurine's neck, and draw up as tightly as possible, overlapping at the back.

Fitting the yoke (D)

24. Measure across from one shoulder to the other to see what size the yoke needs to be to cover up all the rough edges of fabric, then cut out the yoke, roughly in the shape of diagram D.

Dip the back yoke into the adhesive, squeeze out the excess, then place it on the back just below the ruff, covering the rough edges, and mould it to the body.

Repeat for the front. The neckline of the front yoke will probably need to be lower and more scooped out than that of the back.

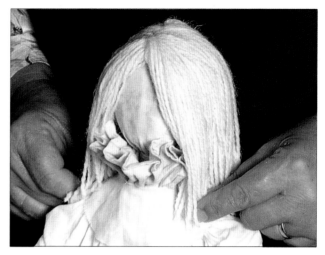

Making the wig

25. You will also need a darning needle. Wind the wool around a piece of thick card, two layers deep. Stitch along the top by back stitching, using a darning-needle, and fasten off. Then cut along the bottom.

26. Holding the wig by the centre parting to prevent tangling, dip it into the adhesive and really soak it. Squeeze out the excess, then place the wig on your almost-completed choirboy, arranging the hair tidily. At this stage the hair will probably be a bit too long.

Finishing off

27. Trim the wig to the desired length – I have left this one fairly long – and tuck the ends of the hair into the ruff to neaten.

This particular wig is straight, because I have used ordinary wool, but I often make curly wigs for my figurines by using bouclé or crimped wool. The choirboys on pages 10–11 have curly hair.

28. Finally, arrange the arms in the required position, bending the elbows and flattening the hands with pliers to accommodate a hymn-book made of a piece of folded card, perhaps with a couple of sheets of folded paper glued inside it to make 'pages'. Do allow the choirboy to dry out completely before gluing the hymn-book into place.

Painting your figurine

The natural calico I have used to make this choirboy actually looks very attractive unpainted, so you could simply varnish the figurine to keep off the dust.

If for any reason you would rather have a figurine in 'naturalistic' colours, you can of course paint it by hand – pink face, red gown, white ruff or whatever. For this you should use acrylic paints as they cover well, have strong colours, and have a resilient finish. Gouache would also be possible. Alternatively, make the gowns and bonnets of fabric in the colours you want and then just varnish.

If, however, you are recycling 'rags', *i.e.* old fabric in an undesirable colour or printed with a pattern you do not wish to see, then spray the figurines with aerosol acrylic car paint. This is what I myself usually do.

You can buy this paint from your local car-spares shop. Usually there is a wide range to choose from, in both plain and metallic colours. If they do not have the colour you require – perhaps you would rather have a more delicate shade – your local art and craft shop may also sell spray craft paints in a variety of colours, or perhaps they can order it for you.

Spray your figurine in a plain colour, or shade it with a couple of similar colours, or try bronzing it.

Bronzing technique

Spray on three coats of dark-brown aerosol acrylic car paint, allowing about thirty minutes between coats. Allow at least one hour to dry.

Then spray some gold, copper or bronze paint on to a small sponge or a piece of rag and drag it just lightly over the surface. If you make a mistake and apply too much gold, simply apply another coat of dark brown. Then allow about an hour's drying time before applying the gold again.

Special note

When spraying with aerosols, it is advisable not to spray in an enclosed area, so do it outdoors if you can. If you must spray indoors, open the windows, and make a spray booth from an old cardboard box to contain the paint.

Options

If you want a 'proper' face and hands for any reason, why not make them out of self-hardening modelling clay (see page 33)?

Spraying the figurine.

Creating a 'bronze' effect with a little metallic paint on a sponge.

The figurine looks very attractive in its
natural calico…

…but you can really go to town
with painting if you like.

Other figurines

Once you have made the basic figurine, you have the knowhow to make a wide range of different figures. The armature and method are essentially the same – just the clothing and accessories vary. You can dress your sculptured figures very simply, or spend as long as you like adding intricate details of collars, cuffs, frills, parasols or whatever your heart desires! As long as your character is wearing some kind of long, draped garment, it will be suitable for this technique.

Try a Nativity scene with the Holy Family, shepherds, kings, angels, etc., all dressed in robes; a witch, wizard or swirling-caped vampire for a children's Hallowe'en-party centrepiece; a small group of carol singers for Christmas; a flower-seller; historical figures such as Queen Elizabeth I or mediaeval damsels; or a veiled bride all in white, with a long, flowing train – you could design her to hold a spray of real flowers on a wedding-party table!

In the following pages I have shown a few suggestions for different designs of figurine and given you the shapes of one or two pattern pieces for them. Half the fun is experimenting and coming up with your own variations on clothes and accessories!

Angel

The angel is very similar to the choirboy – just add a pair of wings and spray her gold for a stunning effect. I have given her a cardboard scroll to hold, but you could also use a golden trumpet or harp, which are often available to hang on Christmas trees.

The pattern for the wings is shown actual size.

Cut wings from a 2-litre (4-pint) plastic bottle and spray them only lightly with gold spray, so that the wings are still slightly transparent. This will give them a gauzy, insubstantial look. Then simply push the pins through the pin-holes on to the angel.

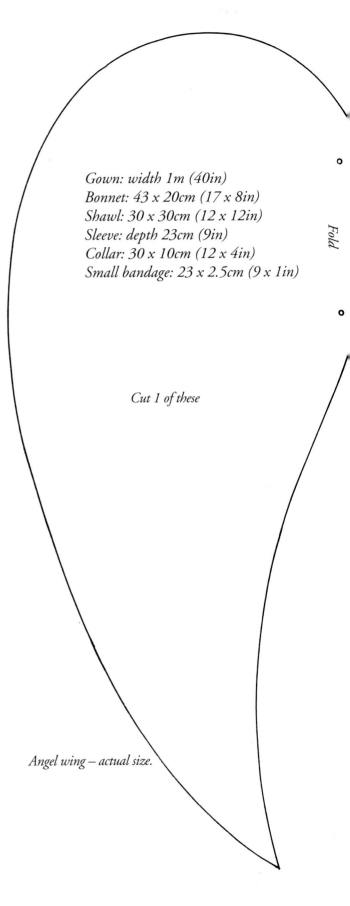

Gown: width 1m (40in)
Bonnet: 43 x 20cm (17 x 8in)
Shawl: 30 x 30cm (12 x 12in)
Sleeve: depth 23cm (9in)
Collar: 30 x 10cm (12 x 4in)
Small bandage: 23 x 2.5cm (9 x 1in)

Fold

Cut 1 of these

Angel wing – actual size.

Shepherd

The shepherd is actually one of the easiest figurines of all to make, with no complicated pattern pieces. This would be a good one for children to make and it always goes down well in schools.

Simply drape the robes around the figure, add a headdress with a band round it, and spray the whole thing brown. Add a wire shepherd's crook for authenticity.

You could, of course, make a whole Nativity scene if you liked.

Victorian-style Father Christmas

Father Christmas was one of the few figurines that I thought really needed a face. This one was simply a hanging Christmas-tree decoration which I used as the head. These are usually made of plastic and are hollow. Alternatively, you could make a head yourself using a small piece of self-hardening or oven-bakeable modelling clay.

To make this figurine, follow the basic instructions for making the choirboy, using the Santa-Claus head in place of the newspaper head. You will also need a wooden plant stick about 30cm long and 1cm thick (11 x ½in). Pierce a hole at the base of the head, making sure that it is the same diameter as the plant stick (it needs to be a tight fit). Push the plant stick in as far as it will go, then apply a little glue around the hole to secure the plant stick. Allow to dry overnight if possible.

Continue making the figurine, following the basic instructions for making the choirboy. When forming the chicken wire, shape it into a cylinder, pinch it in at the neck to secure the head, and then, at about waist level, squeeze it in a little to form a slight waistline. Follow the choirboy pattern shapes A and B (robe and sleeve), reducing the fullness of the robe by 25cm (10in). Then drape the robe around the armature as usual.

To make a hood, cut an 18cm (6in) square of cotton sheeting or calico and attach it to the gathered robe. Roll the front of the hood back a little, and arrange it until you like the way the folds fall. Then attach the sleeves, following the choirboy instructions.

When the figure is dry, spray the robe red, masking out the face with a piece of plastic bag tucked well into the crevices of the hood. I have also brushed on a little white paint with a dry brush to indicate a dusting of snow, but this is an optional effect – the figure looks perfectly good in plain red.

For the sack, cut a 18cm (6in) square of cotton sheeting or calico and sew to form a sack. Fill out with tissue paper when it is still wet to allow the toys to fit in later. Take out the tissue paper when the sack is dry. Colour the sack dark brown, then glue it on Father Christmas's shoulder and fill it with a selection of colourful miniature wooden toys (sold as Christmas-tree decorations).

This figurine would look good displayed as a Christmas centrepiece with perhaps a toy sledge, some cotton wool or wadding for snow, and a miniature artificial fir tree or two.

Victorian lady

This is just one of the many historical costume figures you can make in this craft. The technique is perfect for rich folds in draperies, cloaks, long, flowing skirts, shawls, etc. The fabric pieces are simple to work out – but the effect is lovely.

To make the Victorian lady, you will need the

materials you used for the choirboy, plus 2m (2¼yd) of 5cm (2in) wide lace and some thick mounting card about 20 x 15cm (8 x 6in) to wind the wool on to (to make the wig).

Bodice

Roughly follow the bodice shape in the pattern below. Place it on the figurine after you have fitted the sleeves.

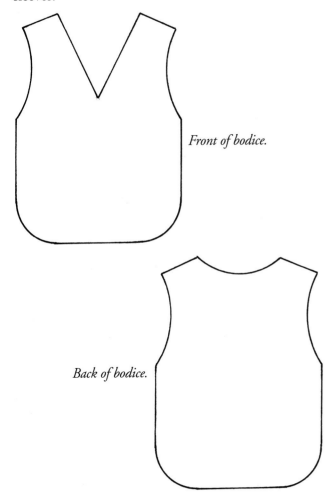

Front of bodice.

Back of bodice.

Sleeves

Cut the sleeve shape as for the choirboy but half the arm length (to allow for a 5cm (2in) cotton lace frill).

Skirt

This should generally be about twice the diameter of the base. Adjust this if you like, according to how full you would like the skirt to be.

Length of skirt

Measure from the waist down and allow for a 5cm (2in) deep cotton lace on the under-skirt and a 5cm (2in) frill on the top skirt, from cotton fabric (adjust accordingly).

Making a parasol

You will need

A 12cm (4¾in) diameter posy frill (from your local florist or craft shop)

A 15cm (6in) diameter cotton doily

A wooden barbecue skewer about 4mm (⅛in) thick and 14cm (5½in) long, or an odd knitting needle of the same size

Small amount of PVA solution – 1 part water, 1 part PVA. Make about a cupful

1. Dip the cotton doily into PVA solution, soak well, squeeze out, and set aside.

2. Next, push the barbecue skewer through the hole in the centre of the posy frill, then take the pre-soaked doily and place it on top of the posy frill, allowing the skewer to protrude through the centre for about 5mm (¼in). Wrap a piece of masking tape around the stick to prevent it slipping through the hole.

3. Stand upright in a tall glass and allow to dry overnight in a warm dry place.

Parasol.

Laundrywoman

More simply dressed than the Victorian lady, the laundrywoman has a bodice made of crossed strips of cloth and an apron. The mob cap is made rather like the handbag on page 39, from a circle of fabric with running stitches round the edge which you then gather.

Her little pile of freshly ironed clothes is made of small pieces of neatly folded fabric.

Balloon seller

The balloon seller is made in a similar manner to the Victorian lady, with her long dress. The bodice shape is the same as that in the pattern on page 27. Also make an apron from a piece of fabric gathered down one side with running stitches plus two strips of cloth for apron ties. The hat is a miniature straw hat I found in a shop.

The balloons are made from five ping-pong balls (table-tennis balls).

Scarlett O'Hara

This glamorous figure involves rather more work – she has a marvellous crinoline with ruffled sleeves and is mounted on a display board (see page 39 for instructions on how to do this). She wears a necklace and carries a miniature basket. The corgi was a final touch – then the whole thing was bronzed.

Knight's lady

Make this figurine in thirteenth-century court dress with a simple high-waisted draped robe, a criss-cross bodice, a tall mediaeval headdress with a cardboard cone as a base, and a long veil made from a piece of old net curtain. Then spray the whole thing in your chosen colour: I have picked lime green.

Bottle-based figurines

This is a really innovative way to use those plastic washing-up-liquid bottles we usually throw away. Filled with sand, they create a perfect foundation for these endearing Beatrix-Potter-style figurines – rather heavier than the wire ones, and perhaps more suitable for children to make, as there is no chicken wire involved that might scratch small hands.

Materials

About 2m (2yd) cotton sheeting or medium-weight calico
PVA glue
An empty plastic bottle about 23cm (9in) tall
Man-size paper tissues
A small tube of glue, or a glue gun
Modelling clay (self-hardening)
Small pots of enamel model paint (pale grey for heads and black for eyes), or artist's acrylics
Small paintbrush
Two cocktail sticks
Needle and strong button thread
Enough sand to fill your plastic bottle
Two lengths of plastic-covered wire – each about 56cm (22in) long
Car spray paint – colour of your choice
28cm x 5mm (11 x $^{1}/_{4}$in) dowelling or plant stick – this should be a tight fit into the top of the bottle

Equipment

Scissors
Snub-nosed pliers
Funnel to fit plastic bottle
Knitting needle (for making the eyes)
Small paintbrush
Turntable or dinner plate

Harvest mouse sprayed bronze for an autumnal look.

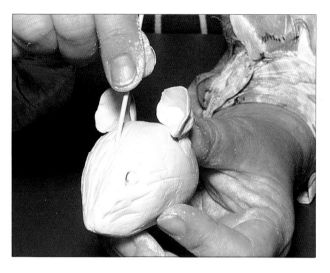

To make the head

1. Start by moulding the self-hardening modelling clay into an egg shape (about the size of a large chicken's egg). Shape one end almost to a point to form a pointed snout and make two eye sockets with the knitting needle.

   Take a small piece of clay, roll it into a ball about 2cm (³/₄in) in diameter, and then cut it in half – one half for each ear. Mould the ears, then graft them on to the head, carefully smoothing out the joins with your finger.

2. For the eyes, roll tiny pieces of clay about the size of small beads into two balls, then push them into the eye sockets. Then take the cocktail stick and stroke the surface from the nose, working toward the back of the head, to give a fur-like appearance.

Note At this point, if you were making the rabbit figurine, you would make a small ball from the clay to form the snout.

Clay collar

3. Roll a ball of clay about 3cm (1¼in) in diameter, squash it flat, put it on to the base of the head, then take the piece of dowelling and push it into the centre of the collar about 3.5cm (1³/₈in), turn it, then pull it out, leaving a small hole for mounting the head later. Set aside.

   Follow the drying instructions on the modelling-clay packet, as they do vary. It is usually about two to three days in a warm dry place.

To make the body

4. Fill the plastic bottle with sand almost to the top, using your funnel, and put the cap back on. You will need to make the hole in the cap large enough to push the dowelling through.

Push the dowelling right to the bottom of the bottle. You should now have a length of dowelling protruding above the top of the bottle.

5. Now cut off the excess, leaving about 3cm (1¼in) protruding from the top of the bottle. When the head is dry, mount it on the stick using a little glue.

Now carry on just as you did for the choirboy: loop the first piece of plastic-covered wire around the neck in exactly the same way as you did before. Repeat until you have an arm at each side, then twist the wires together all the way along each arm.

An easy way to measure the arm is to bend where you think the shoulder would be, then the elbow, then measure to the fingertips and cut off any excess wire.

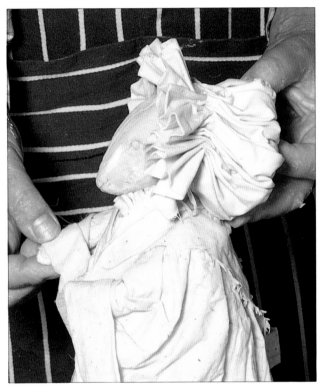

6. Continue to dress the figurine just as you did for the choirboy, then add a simple shawl made from a triangle of fabric. The finishing touch is a ruched bonnet made rather like the ruff (see pattern opposite). Draw up the strings tightly and carefully, tuck the back of the bonnet in neatly to form the proper shape, and arrange the gathers round the face. Finally, tie the threads tightly under the chin and cut the ends off to neaten.

Spray as usual, then paint the face grey or soft brown. Accessories could include little baskets – the rabbit has some knitting in hers – while the mouse wears a pair of tiny spectacles made from looped wire and carries a miniature candle and book.

Pattern pieces for bottle-based figurines

Before you start cutting out the cloth pieces, you will need to take a few measurements. They will obviously vary according to the size of the bottle.

Starting with the gown measurement, i.e. the length, take the plastic bottle and measure from the top to the base, then add about 5cm (2in) (for the hem), then work out the width measurement to give a reasonable fullness when the gown is fitted..

For the sleeves, measure from the top of the shoulder to the paw tips, then add about 6cm (2³/₄in) for the hem.

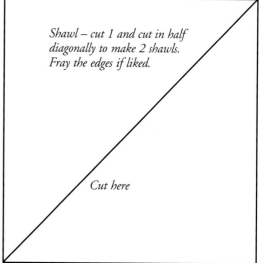

Shawl – cut 1 and cut in half diagonally to make 2 shawls. Fray the edges if liked.

Cut here

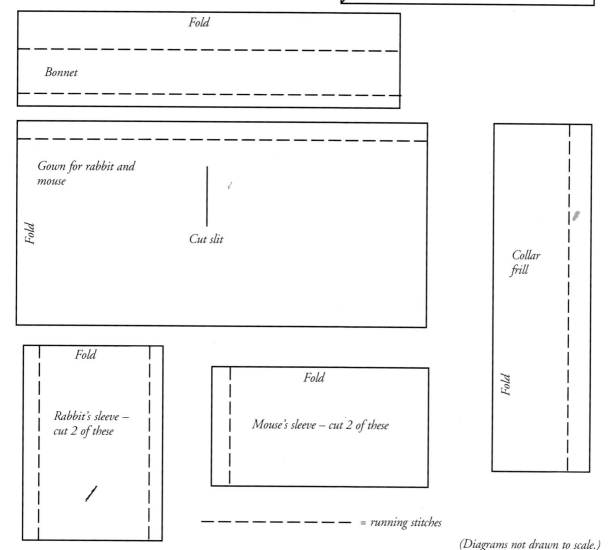

Fold

Bonnet

Gown for rabbit and mouse

Fold

Cut slit

Collar frill

Fold

Fold

Rabbit's sleeve – cut 2 of these

Fold

Mouse's sleeve – cut 2 of these

– – – – – – – – – – = running stitches

(Diagrams not drawn to scale.)

Woodland figurines.

Displaying the animal figurines

These figurines would look lovely in a child's room, especially if you make a little set to display them in. This one was made of three pieces of stout cardboard hinged with tape at the joins and papered with a small-scale wallpaper (a dolls'-house wallpaper would also be suitable). I then added a border, a tiny framed picture, and a 'window' decorated with stiffened fabric-sculpture curtains which I painted blue. You could also try your hand at making fabric-sculpture armchairs and sofas with draped stiffened fabric.

The finished mouse before painting.

An alternative colour scheme for the mouse, each piece of the clothing, head and paws individually painted with acrylic paints.

Accessories for the figurines

There are two options here: making them yourself out of self-hardening modelling clay, plaster, wood, scraps of lace and bits and pieces, or, where this is not possible or sensible, tracking them down. Collecting accessories can be quite exciting!

Craft fairs and village fêtes may have bric-à-brac stalls providing a treasure trove for the craft-minded: odd bits of cotton lace, old bead necklaces, odd silk flowers, balls of wool, etc. Other possible sources are Christmas bazaars, fundraising events such as jumble sales; market stalls (for straw hats and baskets); cake-decorating specialist shops (for tiny silk flowers); dolls'-house shops; antique shops that sometimes have bargain boxes outside (I found the little corgi dog pictured with Scarlett in a bargain box – it had a slight chip on the right leg but as I was going to spray it anyway it did not matter in the least); or charity shops.

A selection of interesting accessories and trimmings for figurines: hats, lace, bows, flowers, beads, baskets and wool for wigs.

Making a drawstring handbag

Simply cut a 13cm (5¼in) circle from calico. Trim it with some narrow lace around the outer edge; then, using button thread, sew small running stitches around the edge about 1.5cm (½in) in. Dip the whole thing into PVA and draw up to form a pouch. Stuff with a tissue, if needed. Make a handle from button thread to hook over the figurine's arm.

Allow to dry as for the parasol on page 27.

Mounting your figurines

I have mounted some of my figurines on to a board for demonstration purposes, but if you like the idea, and would like to mount your figurine, you will need a thick cake board from a cake-decorating shop, larger than your figurine, and a box of external filler with a strong adhesion.

Following the manufacturers' instructions, make up enough filler to cover your board: the layer should be about 2.5cm (1in) thick in the centre and should taper towards the edges. Your figurine should be completely dry, and uncoloured if possible. If you coloured it before you decided to mount it, do make sure the paint is dry.

When you have completely covered the cake board and while the filler is still wet, carefully pick up your dry figurine and place it in position. Push it down firmly and then make sure it stays in that position for a few hours. Allow to dry according to the instructions on the pack.

When it is completely dry, spray the whole thing in the desired colour.

Mounting your figurine on to a board.

Decorative accessories for the home

There is more to this craft than figurines! You can also make a wide range of super accessories to decorate your home, from candlesticks and baskets to garlands and vases. The techniques are no more difficult than those you have just learnt.

Vase with tassels

This particular shape of vase is excellent for displaying pampas grass, tall dried plant material, or silk flowers. Should you want to display fresh plant material, simply cut the top off a lemonade bottle, half fill it with water to weigh it down, then place it inside the vase as a liner.

Materials

A plastic sweet jar
Two pieces of muslin measuring about 1 sq m (1 sq yd)
About 1 litre (2 pints) of diluted PVA solution
A bag of sand (1.5kg or about 3lb)
Black spray paint (car spray or hobby paint)
Gold spray paint

Button thread
A piece of stiff card approximately 13 x 10cm (5 x 4in)
A ball of parcel string

Equipment

Tape measure
Scissors
A large piece of plastic (to protect your work surface)
Large needle

Note Measurements for the muslin are based on a plastic sweet jar 50 x 30cm (25 x 12in). If you have a different size or shape jar, follow the same technique, but cut the muslin according to the size of your jar.

1. Take the pre-cut squares of muslin and place one on top of the other. Now tack the squares together all around the edge and fasten off.

Next, dip them into the PVA solution. Soak well, squeeze them out, then lay them on top of the protected work surface. Then take your plastic sweet jar and place it in the centre of the muslin. Take each corner and pull up tight to the top of the jar, forming the folds as you go. Tuck the muslin into the top of the jar.

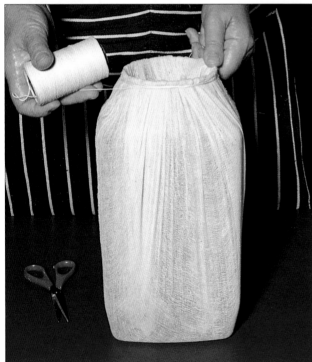

2. Measure 1cm (¼in) below the top of the jar. Take the button thread, wind it around two or three times, and fasten off as tight as you can.

3. Now take the excess muslin from the inside of the jar and pull it up and over the sides. Then scrunch it up to hide the string, tucking under any untidy ends. If you find the muslin has dried out a little, add more PVA solution.

Making the tassels

1. Take the stiff card and wind the string around it from one side to the other. Do this twice. Measure out a length of string about 120cm (48in) long. Fold it in half, then start to twist to the end, forming a sort of rope.

Thread the string rope through the top of the card, then loosely tie the rope together, just to hold it.

2. Now, with your scissors, cut the string across the bottom of the card.

3. Lift off the card carefully. Now tie the string rope very tightly.

4. About 2.5cm (1in) from the top of your tassel, tie a piece of string, again very tightly, to form the top knot. Continue winding down for about 2cm (³/₄in), then tie off, keeping it neat. Repeat, to make up the pair.

5. Dip the tassels into PVA solution, soaking them well, and squeeze out, then tie them around your vase just above the shoulders. Arrange them at different levels for a more stylish effect. Finally, spray the whole vase in your chosen colour.

Mirror

No one would ever believe that this mirror is made from old fabric, MDF (medium-density fibreboard) and string!

The backing board is actually made of 1.5cm ($\frac{1}{2}$in) thick MDF. The gleaming folds are, of course, crumpled fabric glued to the base, giving the effect of plaster moulding, while the mirror edging is a length of cotton cord. The tassels are also made of string, using the same method as on page 42.

Once everything is assembled, carefully mask out the mirror and then spray the whole thing bright gold. A designer mirror at minimal cost!

For a dramatic look, try spraying it black, highlighted in silver, or for a bedroom mirror add a few silk roses and spray it pink. You could pick out small details, such as the tassels, in a contrasting paint colour to tone in with your décor (use artists' acrylic paints).

Calico candlesticks

These candlesticks can be sprayed a different colour every time you change your dining-room décor! They are also an interesting and useful way of recycling film-cassette cases, which always look as if they ought to come in handy for something but usually end up being thrown away.

To make a pair of candlesticks, you will need the following items:

Materials

PVA solution, 1 part water, 1 part PVA. Make up about 500ml (1 pint)
Calico, approximately 92 x 46cm (36 x 18in)
Two pieces of wooden dowelling or broomstick, 18cm x 2.5cm (7 x 1in)
Two plastic film-cassette cases with lids
Strong button thread
Sewing thread for sewing machine
A piece of medium-thickness card (from a cereal box) for the candlestick bases
A small amount of kitchen foil for lining the candle cup
A small selection of odd silk flower heads, or perhaps beads, or dried cones, etc.

Equipment

Scissors
Glue gun or a tube of strong glue
Sewing machine if you have one
Jam jar for mixing PVA
Small bowl for PVA

To make the frilled candlestick base

1. Take one calico base piece 82 x 16cm (32 x 6½in) and sew up both ends to form a circle. (Use a sewing machine, or sew by hand in small running stitches, which will take a little longer.) Back stitch at both ends to secure. Turn right side out and fold over. To prevent twisting, you can either pin the two sections together or tack them with sewing thread (not button thread).

Then measure about 2.5cm (1in) down from the top edge. Using button thread, sew running stitches about 1cm (½in) long around the circle. Do not fasten off, as you will be drawing it up to form a frill. Repeat for the other candlestick base.

Take the first calico strip (*i.e.* the candlestick cover) and fold in half lengthwise. Sew to form a tube. Fasten at both ends and turn right side out. Then, using the button thread, sew running stitches around the top and bottom. Take out the needle, but leave the button thread loose because we will be drawing the ends up at the next stage. Repeat for the other candlestick cover.

Now glue the lid of the film cassette case to the length of dowelling or broomstick, then glue the film-cassette case firmly to the glued-on lid. Check that the hole in the centre of the frill is the right size to take the dowelling.

2. Then dip the candlestick cover into PVA. Soak well, squeeze out, and slide on to the dowelling. Draw up both ends, pull taut lengthwise, and simply twist until you have the desired folds.

3. You may find that the calico is too long at the bottom. If so, trim it to the level of the stick. For the top, take out the button-thread running stitches and tuck the excess inside the film-cassette case.

4. Dip the calico base into PVA, soak well, squeeze out, and draw it up to form a frill, leaving a hole in the middle for the dowelling. Slide the frill over the dowelling, approximately 2cm (³/₄in) along. Then draw up very tightly, tie off, and either arrange the frill in even folds or twirl it like a Catherine wheel, depending on the effect you would like.

Now cut a small rectangular piece of card to fit round the inside walls of the cassette, cover it with kitchen foil and insert it in the top, where the candle will eventually go. This will stop the candle setting fire to the candlestick if it is ever allowed to burn down too far, and will also hold the excess calico in place and neaten the top.

Allow to dry in a warm dry place for about two days. Then cut a circle about 1cm (³/₈in) smaller than the base of the candlestick from medium-thickness card and glue it to the base. Wait until both candlesticks are completely dry before decorating them.

5. To cover the join at the base, glue on silk flower-heads, beads, pine cones, artificial berries, etc., using a glue gun or any other clear strong glue. If you do not want to colour your candlesticks, do make sure you apply a protective coating of clear acrylic car spray. Give them two applications and allow thirty minutes between each coat. It is quick-drying and gives you a really hard finish.

Calico baskets

These attractive baskets look lovely filled with artificial or fresh flowers, nuts or fruit, or perhaps selected pebbles or fir cones. They are so simple to make – an imaginative way of using new or used plastic plant pots.

Choosing plastic plant pots

To make your basket an appropriate shape, remember to choose a plastic flowerpot that is fairly shallow, whatever the diameter. I have based the larger basket on a pot 19cm (7½in) in diameter x 15cm (6in) high and the smaller basket on a pot 16.5cm (6½in) in diameter x 9cm high (3½in). These were used plastic plant pots that were originally bought from my local garden centre with bulbs in them.

You can also cut down taller pots to the right proportions if you cannot find the shallower ones, or use a large margarine tub or ice-cream container.

All shapes are based on the larger basket. To make the smaller basket, follow the instructions for the larger basket and simply scale everything down to suit a small pot.

To make the little bows on the side of the smaller basket, follow the technique for making the garland bow (see pages 55–56), simply scaling down the size.

Flower-arranging

If you want to arrange fresh flowers in your basket, line your basket with a plastic bowl or perhaps the bottom half of a plastic lemonade bottle, or a jam jar half filled with water.

Otherwise just put some artificial flowers in it. To arrange artificial flowers, fill a plastic bag with sand, place it in the basket, and arrange your flowers. This also helps the stability of the basket.

Equipment

Scissors
Rolling pin
Paper fasteners
Plastic bowl (for mixing the PVA)
A fine knitting needle

Materials

Calico approximately 120 x 120cm (48 x 48in)
Plastic plant pot approximately 19cm (7½in) in diameter x 15cm (6in) high
Strong button thread and needle
Piece of medium-thickness card approximately 20cm (8in) square (for base)
PVA – make up about 500ml (1 pint): 1 part water to 1 part PVA, well mixed
A 1-litre (2-pt) plastic lemonade bottle (to cut up to make the handle)
Aerosol car-spray paint
For bronzing: 1 can dark brown
                  1 can gold
For the iridescent basket:
                  1 can pearl blue
                  1 can pearl green
Pencil for marking pattern pieces
Gold calligraphy marker for highlighting (optional)

Small basket.

Pattern pieces for calico baskets

(Diagrams not drawn to scale.)

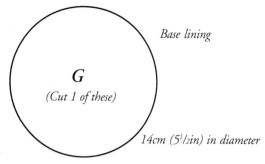

Base lining

G
(Cut 1 of these)

14cm (5¹/₂in) in diameter

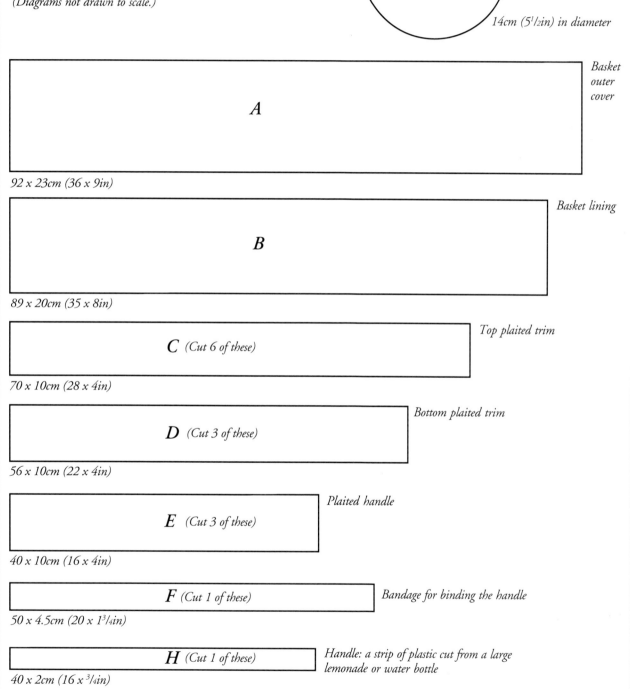

Basket outer cover

A

92 x 23cm (36 x 9in)

Basket lining

B

89 x 20cm (35 x 8in)

Top plaited trim

C (Cut 6 of these)

70 x 10cm (28 x 4in)

Bottom plaited trim

D (Cut 3 of these)

56 x 10cm (22 x 4in)

Plaited handle

E (Cut 3 of these)

40 x 10cm (16 x 4in)

F (Cut 1 of these)

Bandage for binding the handle

50 x 4.5cm (20 x 1³/₄in)

H (Cut 1 of these)

Handle: a strip of plastic cut from a large lemonade or water bottle

40 x 2cm (16 x ³/₄in)

49

Making a large basket

1. Start by cutting the calico strips required: A, B, C, D, E, F, and G. To avoid mixing them up, mark each piece with the appropriate letter in pencil, close to the edge of the calico. Take the calico strips marked A and B. Lay the plant pot on its side. Now dip the outer cover (A) into the PVA mixture and squeeze out the excess. Lay it across the plant pot. Form the calico into folds all the way around the plant pot, as shown in the photograph, then fold under at the bottom and in at the top. Stand the pot upright. Take piece B and dip into PVA mixture. Squeeze out the excess, and smooth round the inside of the pot to form a lining. Keeping the top tidy, make one or two folds around the inside to make the lining fit. Dip the base lining into the PVA mix, squeeze out the excess and place it inside the basket.

The handle

2. When you have fully covered the pot inside and out with the wet calico, stand it upright and mark the centre of the top. Then, with a fine knitting needle, make a hole 1.5cm ($\frac{1}{2}$in) down from the top on each side of the pot.

Next, take a strip of plastic (H) cut from a plastic water or lemonade bottle. Make a hole with a fine knitting needle 2cm ($\frac{3}{4}$in) from each end. Take one of the paper fasteners and push it through from the outside of the pot to the hole in the handle and fasten by spreading its 'legs' out. Repeat for the other side.

3. Now bind the handle with calico strips (F) and fasten at the base of the handle on both sides.

Plaited trim for handle

4. Take section E (three strips), dip each strip in the PVA mix and squeeze out the excess, then lay the strips flat on a table and fold in the edges to neaten. Repeat for the three strips, and fold into a 2·5cm (1in) wide strip. Tie all three together with button thread, then plait to the end and tie again to secure. Using a rolling pin, flatten the plait.

Carefully lay the plait over the handle and secure by winding button thread around and along it. Tie off at both ends.

Plaited trims for basket

5. Using the six strips labelled C, make two sets of plaits following the instructions above. Apply to the top of the basket and secure by joining with button thread. Tie off. Repeat using pattern piece D, attaching it round the bottom of the basket, then set the basket aside to dry for about two or three days in a warm place such as an airing cupboard or a warm kitchen.

When the basket is completely dry, cut a cardboard circle slightly smaller than the base and glue this in position on the bottom of the basket to hide the fabric edges.

Colouring

Whatever you have chosen for your base colour, you will need at least three applications. Allow about thirty minutes between each application. Then, with the gold spray paint, spray a small amount on to a piece of rag or sponge, then drag it across the plaiting. This will give an almost antique finish to your basket.

Should you wish to decorate your basket on the outside, as I have, you will need a few artificial berries. Also, you may wish to highlight the plaiting with a touch of gold calligraphy pen, which does finish it off rather well.

Plaited garland

This was inspired by a glance in a baker's shop window. Calico and straw are the basic ingredients for this unusual garland.

Materials

A small bag of straw (try a pet shop or garden centre)
Three strips of calico about 150 x 20cm (60 x 8in)
A 5cm (2in) paintbrush
About 1 litre (2 pints) of PVA solution
A large piece of plastic sheeting or some newspapers to protect the work surface
Strong button thread or a reel of sewing thread for a sewing machine
Two cardboard loo-roll tubes

Equipment

Scissors, needle, sewing machine
Glue gun if you have one, or a tube of strong glue
Rolling-pin 5cm (2in) in diameter for pushing straw down the calico tubes, or a wooden spoon
One can of dark-brown aerosol car spray, one can of gold, or a hobby paint.

Helpful hints

You may wish to colour-coordinate one or two projects in the book: for example, a bronzed garland and bronzed candlesticks would complement one another. Alternatively, you may decide on a more delicate look, such as pastel colours brushed with gold.

Colours are, of course, very much a personal choice. Whatever you choose, do try different ideas. You will find that one project often inspires another.

When filling the calico tubes with straw, to avoid the straw making a mess if you are working indoors, you could work over the top of a large dustbin bag, which will collect any stray pieces of straw.

You may find that you have some PVA mix left. This is because some calicos and other cotton-based fabrics are less absorbent than others. Do not worry; the mixture will keep in an airtight jar for about three months.

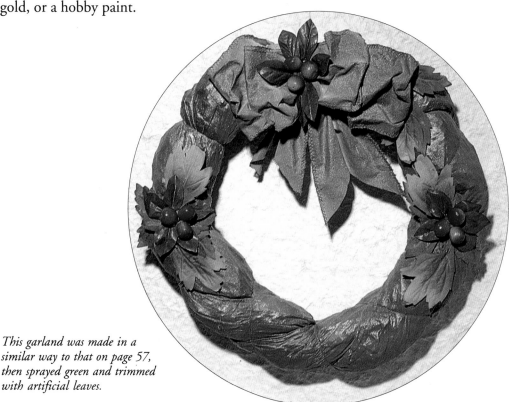

This garland was made in a similar way to that on page 57, then sprayed green and trimmed with artificial leaves.

Making the garland

1. With a sewing machine if you have one, sew the strips of calico lengthwise (seam allowance approximately 1cm (⅜in)) to form three tubes and turn them right side out. Then, about 10cm (4in) down from the top of the tube, tie some button thread really tightly, wind it around two or three times, and tie off.

To fill the tubes, take a handful of straw at a time, then, with the wooden spoon or rolling pin, push the straw down the tube. Try not to pack it too tightly. Repeat until you have filled it to about 10cm (4in) from the end, then secure with button thread.

Repeat until you have filled and tied at both ends all three tubes.

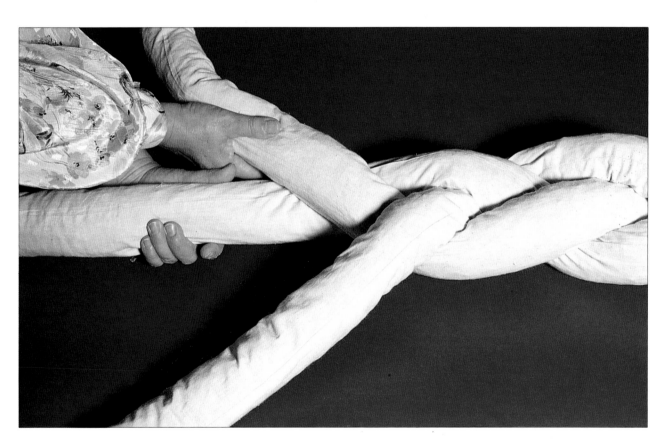

2. Tie the three tubes together at one end only. Now find a door handle or the back of a chair, or get someone to hold the tied ends of the tubes for you, then begin to plait all three together. Plait fairly tightly from one end to the other. Tie the ends together with thread, then form the plait into a circle. Bind the ends together as neatly as you can with button thread. Do not worry too much if it is not as neat as you would like, as the bow will eventually cover any imperfections.

3. Next you will need the prepared PVA mix and the 5cm (2in) paintbrush. Decide which side of your garland you would like to be the front, then turn the front face down on to your work top and paint on the PVA mix, making sure that you work the mixture into the folds.

Repeat on the other side. Set aside until you have completed the bow.

Garland bow

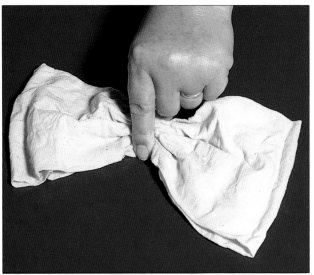

4. Pour the remainder of the PVA mixture into a medium-sized bowl. Then cut two strips of calico, one about 63 x 25cm (25 x 10in) (for the bow) and the other 50 x 25cm (20 x 10in) (for the bow's tail).

Take the first strip and dip it into the PVA. Soak it well, then squeeze it out, lay it flat on the worktop, and fold the two long edges toward the centre. Next, take the two ends and fold them into the centre, overlapping them slightly. Pinch the strip in the middle to form a bow shape.

5. Take the second strip and dip it into the PVA. Soak it well, squeeze it out, and lay it flat on the worktop, then fold the two long edges toward the centre.

Then lay this strip across the bow and fold it over the top. Push the bow and its tails generally into shape. Trim the ends of the tails into an inverted V if you like.

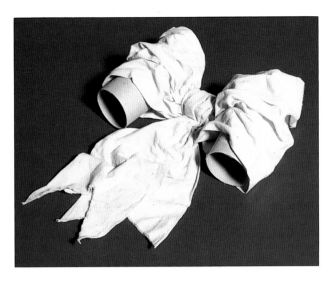

6. To form the 'knot', sew a few running stitches just below where the knot should be, using the button thread. Tie off at the back of the bow, pulling quite tightly.

Take the empty loo-roll tubes and push one through each bow loop. This will help give the bow a better shape and will keep the loops in position until they are dry and can retain their shape.

Note Place the bow and the garland separately on a plastic-lined tray or board and leave to dry for approximately two days in a warm dry place.

When your garland and bow are completely dry, glue the bow into place. Then spray in a colour of your choice, using car spray paint or hobby spray paint to achieve an even finish.

You will usually need to apply two coats of base colour, and normally one coat of gold if you are bronzing. Allow at least two hours between applications.

Decorating your garland

Having glued the bow on to the wreath to hide the join, decorate the garland with silk or dried flowers; dried material such as ears of wheat, pine cones, beech nuts, or dried orange and lemon slices; or artificial berries and fruits.

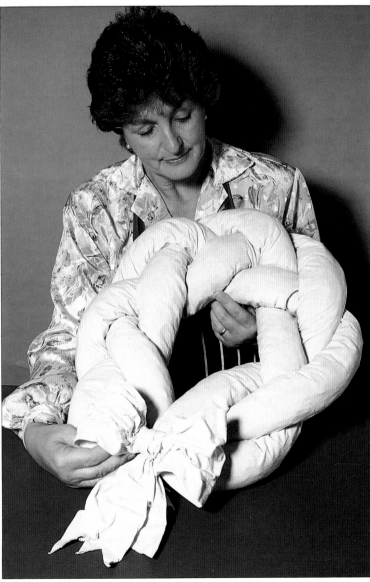

The garland before colouring and decorating.

The finished garland.

Calico cabbages

These are a realistic addition to a harvest-festival arrangement, or fun accessories for the kitchen.

To display them, simply add them to a basket lined with straw and a small selection of vegetables: artificial, if you have them, or alternatively you can use fresh ones, but for a few days only, due to possible moisture problems.

Materials
Two well-shaped medium-sized fresh cabbages
1.5m (1¾yd) calico
PVA solution: 1 part water to 1 part PVA
Small reel of plastic-covered wire
Button thread and needle
Newspaper
Pencil for marking
A 5cm (2in) paintbrush
1 can of dark-green spray paint
1 can of light-green spray paint

Equipment
Rolling pin
Scissors
Small plastic bowl
Two wire coat-hangers
Plastic sheeting to protect work surface

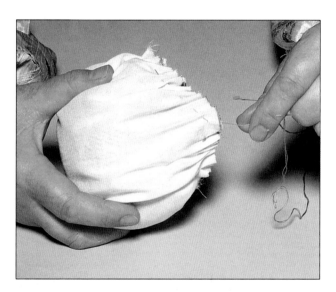

To make the heart of the cabbage
1. Cut a circle of calico approximately 25cm (10in) in diameter and sew small running stitches around the outside edge about 1cm (³⁄₈in) from the edge, using button thread. Do not fasten off. Then take some newspapers and screw them up into a ball about the size of a large orange. Set this aside. Place the calico circle over the newspaper ball and draw the thread up really tightly, then fasten off. Next, paint the calico ball all over with the PVA (be quite liberal), allowing it to soak in well, and set it aside.

2. Take the first cabbage and begin by carefully cutting four leaves from the outer layer, from the base of the cabbage, then four leaves from the second layer. Now take the second cabbage and, again from the base, cut a further four leaves. Set aside. You should now have twelve leaves.

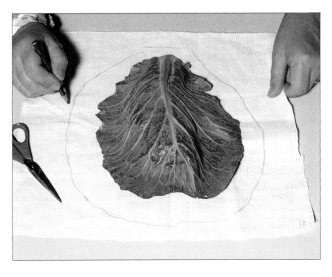

3. Now take one of the cabbage leaves, lay it on top of the calico, and roughly draw an outline in pencil all the way around, slightly larger than the actual leaf. Repeat for the other eleven leaves.

4. Keep each green cabbage leaf with its roughly matching pre-cut calico 'leaf'. Now take one green leaf and place it on the worktop with the outside of the leaf facing you. Then take the matching calico leaf and dip it into the PVA solution. Soak it well, then squeeze it out and lay it on top of the green leaf. Work the calico into the veins. You should start to see the impression of the veins coming through. To help, use the rolling pin, rolling backwards and forwards. If the leaves are more concave than flat, pad them out with paper or a cloth to avoid splitting them and use a brush to work the calico into the veins.

Repeat until you have completed all twelve leaves. Do not worry too much about the sizes of the leaves, as they can be cut to size when dry.

5. Pierce a small hole in the base of each pair of leaves, then cut twelve varying lengths of the plastic-covered wire, the shortest being about 15cm (6in). Take the first length of wire, push it through the pierced hole, then form a hook at both ends. Repeat for all twelve leaves, then hang on the wire coat-hanger to dry. This will take approximately two days in a warm dry place, with the temperature not less than 25°C (77°F). To dry the cabbage heart, pierce the base with a length of wire. Then hang on a separate coat-hanger. Dry at the same temperature as the leaves, and for the same drying period.

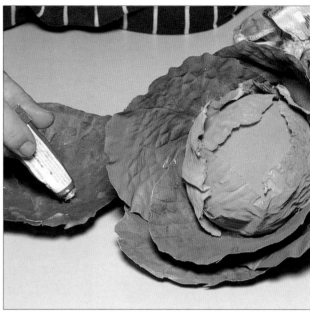

6. When both the leaves and the cabbage heart are completely dry, unhook them, then begin to peel off the green leaves. You should now have some perfect calico leaves (do not throw the wires away as you will be using them again).

Then trim the first four leaves. Trim the second four leaves a little smaller, and the third set of four a little smaller still. These will be layered around the heart when they have been coloured.

Now rethread them on the wires and hook them back on to the coat-hangers. With the can of dark green paint, spray four leaves at a time, spreading them out along the hanger. If possible, do the spraying in the garden, perhaps suspending the coat-hanger from the clothes line. Allow about thirty minutes between each application. Colour all the leaves dark green, including the cabbage heart. Apply two coats of the dark-green paint. Next, take the four smallest leaves and the cabbage heart and overspray with light-green paint – just one application.

You may like to experiment with various shades of green. This is all part of the fun.

Assembling the calico cabbage

7. When you are happy with the colour, assemble the cabbage. First, if the leaves have not curled enough at the edges, curl them over the blade of a pair of scissors.

Glue the first leaf at the base of the cabbage heart using neat PVA glue and a brush, and repeat with the four smallest leaves, overlapping as you go.

Follow the same procedure with the rest of the leaves, checking that all leaves are well glued. To dry, place the cabbage in a pudding basin or a deep dish in a warm dry place overnight.

If you want to reproduce the natural bloom of a fresh cabbage, dust your sculpture with a little talcum powder.

At a glance, the calico cabbage is incredibly realistic!

More ideas

There are lots of other things you can make using the techniques of this fascinating craft! For example, try making a set for a model railway...hills, tunnels, rivers, lakes...all on a base of crumpled chicken wire and old fabric, stiffened and then sprayed in greens and browns, with hedges and woods added. A little boy would also love a sculptured landscape with roads and roundabouts for his toy cars!

Stiffened bows look good on their own, attached to wicker wastepaper baskets, in Christmas holly wreaths and for hanging pictures on ribbons. Or make super larger-than-life fabric flowers – giant tropical blossoms, or lilies, or hibiscus – all stiffened with PVA and sprayed in bright exotic colours.

Classic fabric-swathed pedestals for flower arrangements are another possibility. Spray them to match your décor.

So you see: simply use your imagination and the possibilities of fabric sculpture are endless.

Suppliers

You should have no problem in obtaining any of the the materials or equipment mentioned in this book, but if you do have difficulty in obtaining any item, please write for further information and an constantly updated list of stockists to the Publishers at the address below.

Search Press Limited,
Wellwood, North Farm Road,
Tunbridge Wells,
Kent TN2 3DR,
England.

Index

A

accessories 38
angel 22–23
animals 32–37

B

balloon seller 29
baskets 48–52
bottle-based figurines 32–37
bow 55–56
bronzing 20

C

cake board 39
calico cabbages 58–61
candlesticks 45
choirboy 10–21

F

fabric 7
figurines 10–39

G

garland 53–57
glue 7

H

handbag 39

K

knight's lady 31

L

laundrywoman 28

M

materials and equipment 7–9
mirror 44
mounting figurines 39
mouse 37

P

painting 7, 20
parasol 26
plaited garland 53–57
PVA 7

R

rabbit 36

S

Scarlett O'Hara 30
shepherd 24
spraying 20

T

tassels 42

V

vase 40–43
Victorian lady 26–27
Victorian-style Father Christmas 25

W

wallpaper adhesive 7, 12
wigs 19
wings 22
wire 7
wool 7

OTHER BOOKS PUBLISHED BY SEARCH PRESS

The Art of Batik: Flowers and Landscapes
Mary Taylor

Using the ancient art of batik the most beautiful designs and pictures can be achieved. In step-by-step demonstrations, Mary Taylor shows exactly how she develops her pictures and wall-hangings – roses, poppies, magnolias, landscapes, seascapes. Her work will inspire any artist.

Candlemaking
David Constable

Packed with ideas and instructions, this complete guide shows how to make a marvellous selection of dipped, moulded, and novelty candles; one-colour and perfumed candles; exotic snakes and dramatic water candles. It also gives ideas for painting and carving.

The Art of Annemieke Mein: wildlife artist in textiles
Annemieke Mein

Annemieke is an internationally recognised textile artist, and many of her innovative and stunning textile studies of flora and fauna are beautifully illustrated in full colour in this book. This unique book will provide inspiration for all those working in textiles, needlecrafts, fabric painting and soft sculpture.

The Art of Painting on Silk: Volumes 1–4
edited by Pam Dawson

Volume 1 is a practical course for the beginner, with clear instructions for the three basic techniques of gutta, watercolour and salt; Volume 2 deals with painting on soft furnishings; Volume 3 contains patterns for fashions; Volume 4 offers a pot pourri of ideas for silk painting, including jewellery, cards, and presents.

A Complete Guide to Silk Painting
Susanne Hahn

This definitive guide to silk painting is a unique treasury of ideas, designs and techniques that follows the 'Silk Road' of discovery from fibre through to fabric, and takes you, step by step, through the different techniques of this craft.

You will find information and advice on materials and equipment and a variety of silk-painting effects, plus many ideas for gift and home-furnishing projects including wall-hangings and pictures. There is also a stunning gallery of designs.

The Craft of Natural Dyeing
Jenny Dean

This excellent guide to natural dyeing offers the craftsperson a successful alternative to synthetic dyes. It shows the possibilities of discovering new sources of colour and the satisfaction of growing, or gathering, natural dyestuffs and then using them to produce good fast colours. Jenny gives clear step-by-step instructions for using onion skins to dye both wool and cotton fibres. She also includes comprehensive and well-illustrated lists of natural dyestuffs that provide a full spectrum of colour.

Inspirational Silk Painting From Nature
Renate Henge

The first part of this book deals with the technical side of silk painting: tools; paints and resists; and composition and colour.

The second part of the book offers a range of photographs with the aim of encouraging silk painters to look for inspiration from the world of nature.

If you are interested in any of the above books, or in any of the art and craft books published by Search Press, please send for a free colour catalogue to

SEARCH PRESS LTD.
Department B
Wellwood, North Farm Road
Tunbridge Wells, Kent TN2 3DR
Tel. (01892) 510850 Fax (01892) 515903

or, if resident in the U.S.A.,
ARTHUR SCHWARTZ & CO. INC.
234 Meads Mountain Road
Woodstock, N.Y. 12498
Tel.: 914 679 4024 Fax: 914 679 4093
Orders, toll-free: 800 669